THE SOCIALLY DYNAMIC ORGANISATION
A New Model of Organisational Design

I0049592

ISBN - Paperback 978-1-9165025-9-8 | eBook 978-1-8380196-0-0

Sea Salt Publishing
Bournemouth, Dorset, UK

Websites:

www.seasaltlearning.com

www.julianstodd.wordpress.com

Contents

Introduction

A strange feature of Organisations is that they cast a massive shadow onto their own future.

The things that we do, the ways that we do them and the successes that we have are all held in the footprint that we land upon the earth. For Organisations, this footprint lies in assets, buildings, Reputation, Hierarchy, products and wealth. It is in the nature of Organisations to accrete both things and ways of doing things.

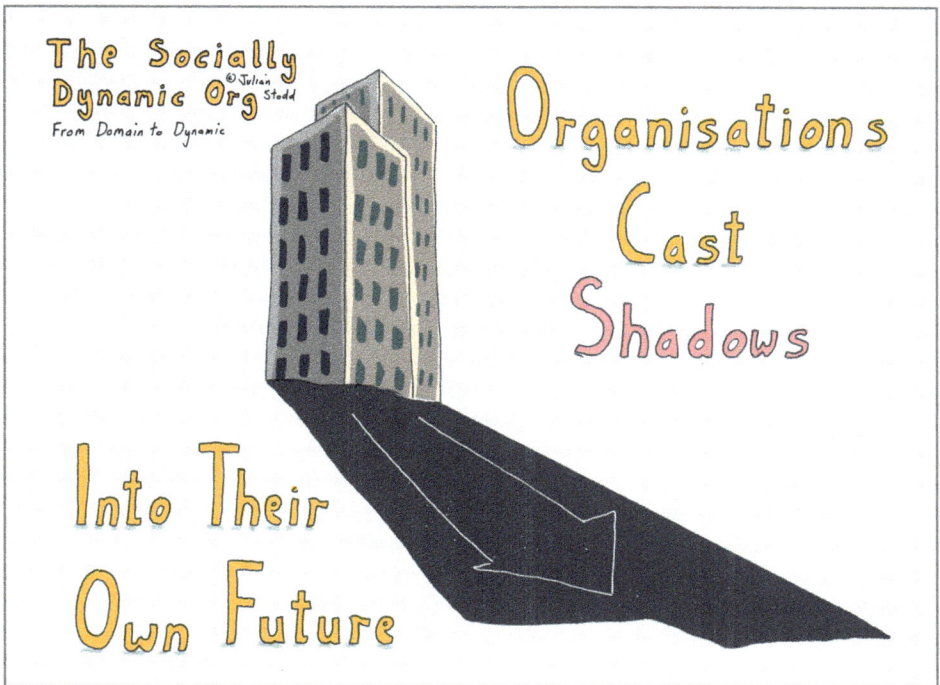

Some of these legacies are huge; hence, the shadows that they cast are long.

But the thing about a shadow is that it should fall away from us. It should fall back into the past, whilst our future lies ahead where we are often blinded by the light.

Our challenge is to create a type of Organisation that respects this legacy but aims firmly towards the future, grounded in the brilliance of its people today.

For a new type of world, we will need a new type of Organisation: one that is lightweight and rapidly adaptable, that thrives in times of constant change, that respects the old but embraces the new.

We need an Organisation that is deeply fair to its people and to the societies within which it operates. We need an Organisation that can change without becoming breathless, is innovative without massive effort and has a high level of engagement because it has earned it.

In other words, we need the impossible: the best of both worlds—an Organisation that is safe and old, yet dynamic and new.

This book paints a picture charting a path from our old 'Domain'-based Organisation to a new type of 'Dynamic' one.

In fact, to a 'Socially Dynamic' one.

My work is set within the context of the Social Age, our evolved ecosystem of operation with its rebalancing of power, emergent social communities, democratisation of technology and interconnected, globally local tribes.

This work explores the intersection of the formal worlds of Hierarchy and the social worlds of Community, and how we can find a new type of Organisation at the boundary between the two.

It is an Organisation that will sit in tension: neither fully formal and visible nor entirely fluid and social.

Not governed solely by system, process, rules and control but, nonetheless, governed.

Creative with structure. Diverse but united. Stronger, yet almost certainly smaller, although that may depend on what exactly you are measuring.

Our task is to understand it, then to build it.

This Book Is Imperfect

This short book is a start, not the end. It's an exploration of the new structure and DNA of the Socially Dynamic Organisation, based upon my writing, work and research, over the last four years or so—the forces that act upon it, the traits that it will exhibit, some aspects of what it will retain and what it will leave behind.

It is not a picture, nor a solution, but rather the early sketched outline. And I have kept it deliberately short, with encouragement to myself and to you to deface these pages, add new chapters and write your own draft.

This is not an instruction manual, nor is it a full-fledged solution. It represents my foundation of understanding, and in some ways, you could view it as a model that sits in the dark. Through each chapter, we will shine a spotlight on one angle, but I am not yet sure we have enough light to illuminate the whole thing.

And this is our challenge: The context of modern operation is not entirely clear, the ecosystem continues to evolve and we must continue doing much of what we have always done. But we must explore; we must sketch out our ideas, ask the unutterable questions and experiment and conceive what will come, once we have exhausted the potential of the old.

Each section covers a different idea. Collectively, they do not form a blueprint but perhaps the imperative against which we will *'architect'* the new.

And these ideas are not final. My understanding of the Socially Dynamic Organisation continues to evolve, and as it does so, some ideas thrive whilst others are subsumed or fade away. And this is as it should be, because of one thing I am sure:

The future Organisation that we inhabit will be the one that we earn, not the one that we buy.

No consultancy, no thought leader, no hero at the top will give us the future.

The Socially Dynamic Organisation will be a story written from within: guided, for sure, but not purely rule-based. Excellent, certainly, but not through system and process alone. It will be built upon the Individual Agency of its own Communities, accountable to its broader Society.

And if we can help take the first steps towards making it a reality, it will be work that makes us proud.

A Practical Guide

Whilst this book is an exploration of ideas, for every section, I have provided a one- or two-line summary of *'what you need to know'*, as well as some questions you can ask yourself or others.

This is one of the principles of the *'Social Age Guidebook'* series: to explore ideas and point into action.

You do not need to read this book in order, or in its entirety, although the final section does paint the most complete summary of how a Socially Dynamic Organisation will look.

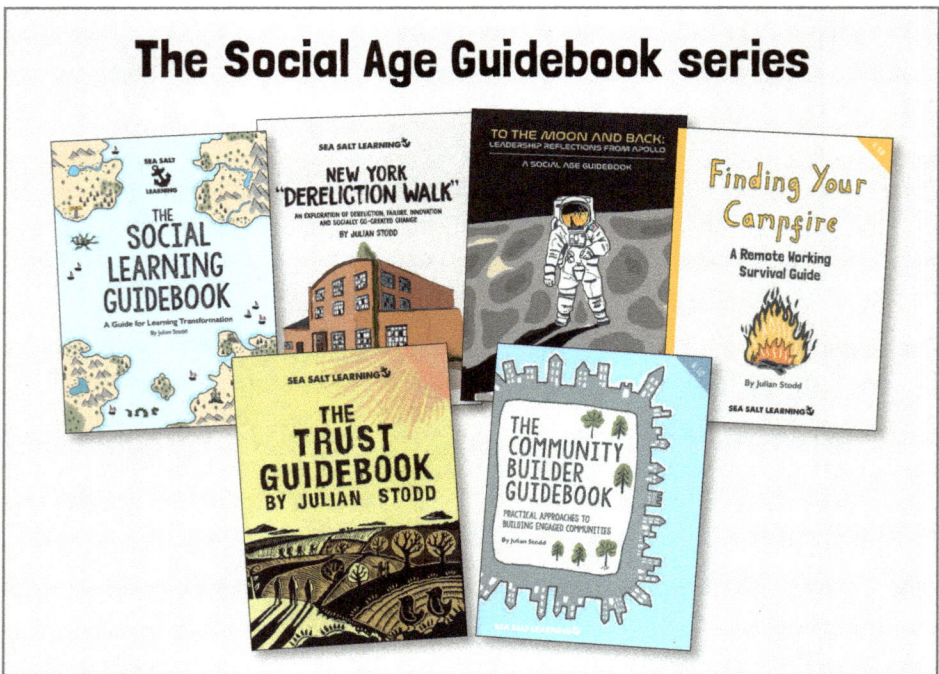

The Social Age Guidebook series

Taking notes

As you read this book you will no doubt come across things that you want to remember or explore further. To help you with this I have added a few notes pages toward the back of the book, so you can remember it at the end.

THE SOCIALLY DYNAMIC ORGANISATION
A New Model of Organisational Design

Part 1

Our Organisations — Domain, Hierarchy and Investment

The design of our Organisations today is largely a legacy of industrial design and the search for effectiveness at scale: a model that has served us well into the Digital Age but may fall short in the Social one.

Let me start by sharing one definition of what a modern Organisation is, as a relic of our industrial heritage, a legacy from a time when geography described the primary location of an Organisation and when transport and communication networks kept it connected to resources and markets.

Within that context, Organisations can be described in two ways: they are entities of collectivism, to achieve an effect at scale.

An Organisation brings together a diverse group of people, according to an overall plan, and uses them to achieve a specific effect on a larger scale. Central to this is that specialism and collective effort can achieve more than an individual or a collection of individuals. It's an additive model. Or, to put it another way, the Organisation houses a lot of people who know a small number of things in depth, not a homogenous group, all of whom know the same thing.

Let me give you an example. If you want to build a house, you need to dig

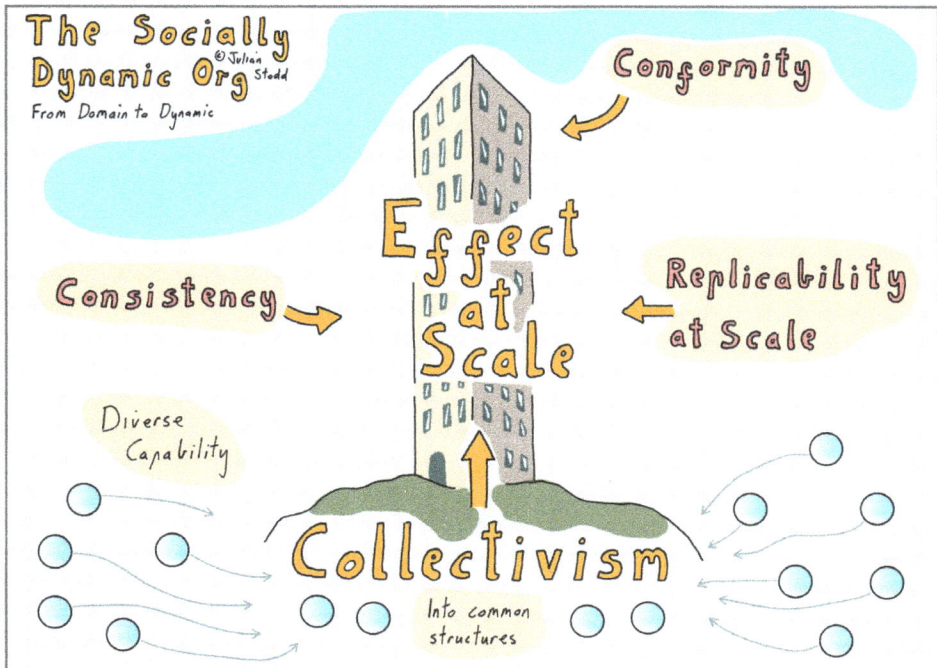

The Socially Dynamic Org
© Julian Stodd
From Domain to Dynamic

Conformity

Effect at Scale

Consistency

Replicability at Scale

Diverse Capability

Collectivism

Into common structures

foundations, build walls, wire up to the grid and put a roof on top. If I can dig holes really well, you may offer me a dollar to dig for a day.

I can't do any of the other things that you need, but I sure as heck know how to dig a good hole. Your ability to build the house is held in your ability to plan effectively (know what size hole you need and that you need an electrician) and to manage the effort.

The people of the Organisation achieve this specific idea of *'effect at scale'* through consistency, conformity and replicability. Consistency is a notion of quality scaled up; conformity is a production value that allows assembly-line motion and handover from one part of the system to the next; replicability allows for globalisation and scale.

In parallel with this, or to achieve this, we end up with Hierarchy and Domains.

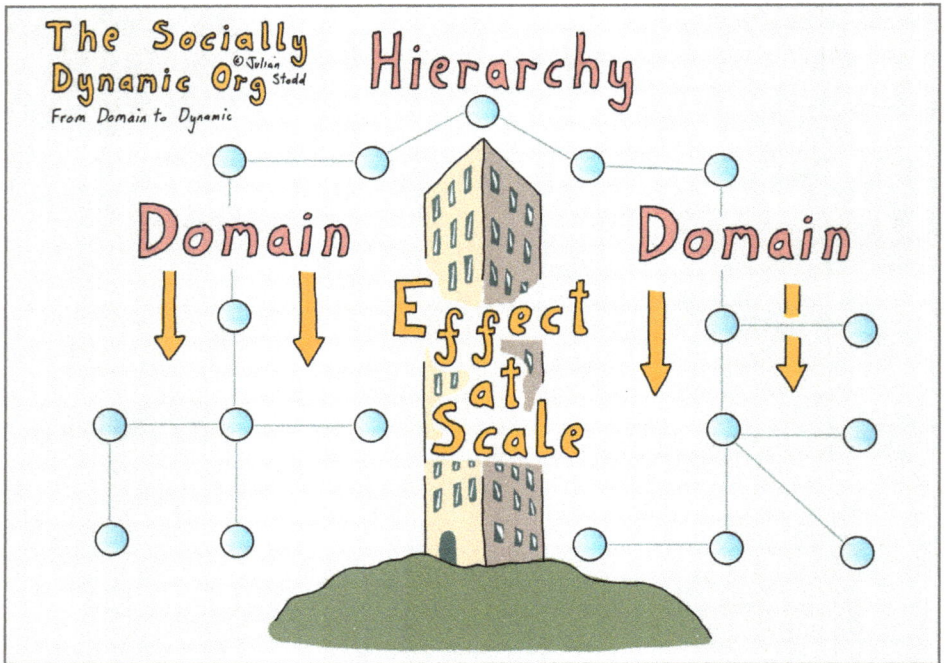

'*Hierarchy*' is a structure to hold power, drive consistency (punish deviation) and achieve conformity (exclude divergence) and replicability (oversight and reporting). I should stress that all of this is a very good thing indeed. This is not about control by megalomaniacs and freaks but, rather, the most sensible mechanisms to drive quality and productivity through distributed systems. After all, if I am digging my hole alongside ten other people, you need to be sure we all have a shovel, and you want to buy the cheapest shovels possible, and you want to be sure that someone is checking how deep the hole I dig is, compared to my partner next door.

'*Domain*' relates to a system of education and empire. We structure our education systems to feed the domains of our dominant Organisational design, and we also nest within these, building out networks and knowledge-based power. Domains are not fluid social structures but, rather, more permanent tribal ones. Examples of our Organisational Domains are HR, IT, Legal, Compliance, Logistics and Retail.

Our Organisations today are structures of Domain, and our primary models of change all attack those Domains.

Once we are invested in a domain through education and tenure, we are invested in maintaining it. This is why I usually say that the constraint we feel in trying to change is held largely by good people doing good work, within systems that radically reward them for continuing to do so without changing. I am on the '*hole digging team*', and you are in the '*managing holes division*'. Let's just say that we have separate Christmas parties.

That is essentially how most Organisations operate. But it's not without its challenges.

One limitation is that the Domains and Hierarchy reflect how we used to build houses, rather than how we hope to build them in the future. If we start to 3D print them or assemble them by drone, the chances are that our collective effort and its management are lacking.

Another limitation concerns my hole. Imagine that I notice that the earth is very sandy, and we would be better off shoring up the sides as we go. Am I going to tell you?

To understand this question better, we should understand the nature of engagement itself and consider this a triangle of utility, time and money. My utility is that I dig holes: you can buy my time by the day for one dollar.

But for one dollar a day, I may not tell you that I can dig a better hole.

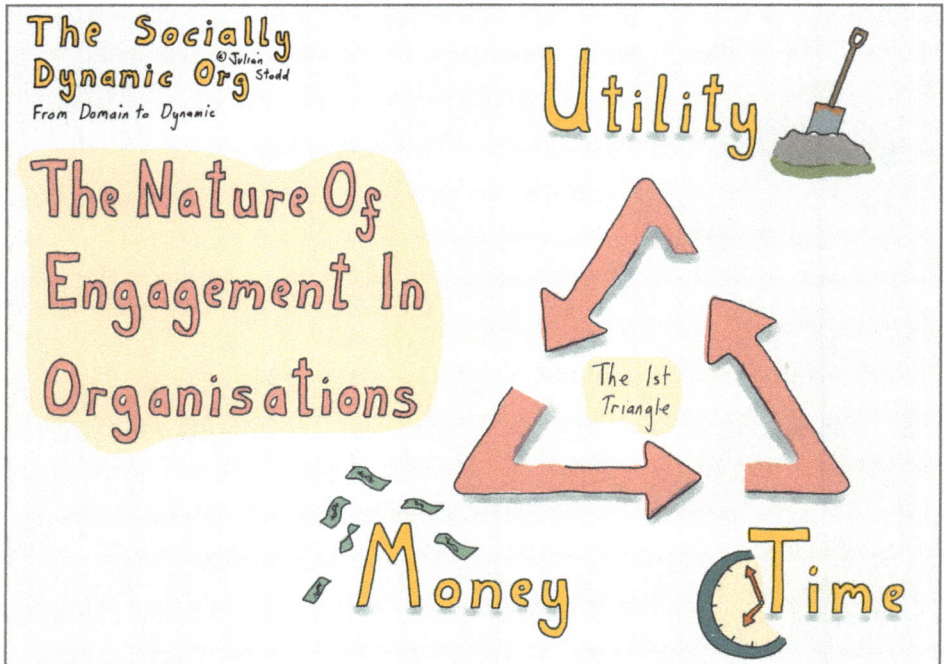

The Socially Dynamic Org ©Julian Stodd
From Domain to Dynamic

The Nature Of Engagement In Organisations

Utility

The 1st Triangle

Money

Time

There is a second triangle, which concerns invested engagement, but the three sides of this have different names: *'Investment'*, *'Reputation'*, *'Opportunity'*. I will choose to invest my ideas if I can build a Reputation and earn a new opportunity.

There may be multiple additional parallel triangles: Investment for Pride and Community, or Investment for Kindness and Gratitude. These are triangles of social currency, and they operate beyond the oversight or control of the Organisation.

I may go home after digging your ineffective hole and dig a hole for my elderly neighbour for free (and shore up the sides), because I feel a sense of community and responsibility. Or because I like them. Or because it seems like the right thing to do. Or because my friends are all helping out, and I want to join them.

The funny thing is that people generally want to invest in the Organisation for which they work, but decades of carelessness have fractured the Social Contract that governs employment, fragmented the ideas of career and demolished the sense of loyalty or a *'job for life'*, in many contexts.

The Socially Dynamic Org © Julian Stodd
From Domain to Dynamic

Investment
Uncertainty Belief

The Other Triangles

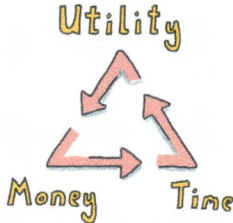

Investment
Reputation Opportunity

Utility
Money Time

Investment
Kindness Gratitude

Investment
Pride Community

It's not to say that we don't like working places, but we are under no illusion that the Organisation comes first.

All this is a way of saying that money does not buy you everything, and indeed, much of what we are likely to need to build a Socially Dynamic Organisation exists beyond money; it trades in other markets.

The very things that we can earn through social engagement are the very things that most Organisations want: 'Collaboration', 'Co-Creation', 'Innovation', 'Change'. To a large extent, all these things are the legacy of discretionary investment, operating in a market beyond money alone.

This idea is a foundation: we need to move away from a pure notion of 'Domain', towards something new, something more Dynamic—in my understanding, something that is Dynamic through the invested engagement and discretionary effort of its people, labouring under a new Social Contract and trading in multiple different economies that we will explore later.

So, a Socially Dynamic Organisation is what comes next. And our task is to build it.

What we need to know

We exist in Domain-based Organisations that have influenced the structures of education and reward that feed them. We operate within hierarchies that keep us safe at the very time when we may need to take on more risk. And we engage people for money when what we increasingly want from them may not be bought.

Questions to ask

1. Is the strength we carry today the strength we need for the future?

2. Does our Hierarchy enable or control?

3. How do we recognise and reward the investment of engagement?

THE SOCIALLY DYNAMIC ORGANISATION
A New Model of Organisational Design

Part 2:

Forces of the Social Age

This Industrial Age paradigm has served us well, building out its distinct Domains—such grounded structures as Logistics, Sales Teams, Estates, Human Resources, Learning and Development, Talent Management, Quality Assurance, Information Technology and Legal, as well as more mobile floating entities such as Agile groups, Coaches, Change teams and Troubleshooters. Still others operate underground: Cleaners, Catering, Postal and Security—the background canvas. And yet others still are bolted onto the side: Research and Development, Innovation Labs, Skunk Works. All the structure of the modern Organisation and, permeating it, a Hierarchy that codifies the power and consequence that enable it to run.

But the model has been eroded by the context of the Social Age. It's removed the value and tipped us off balance.

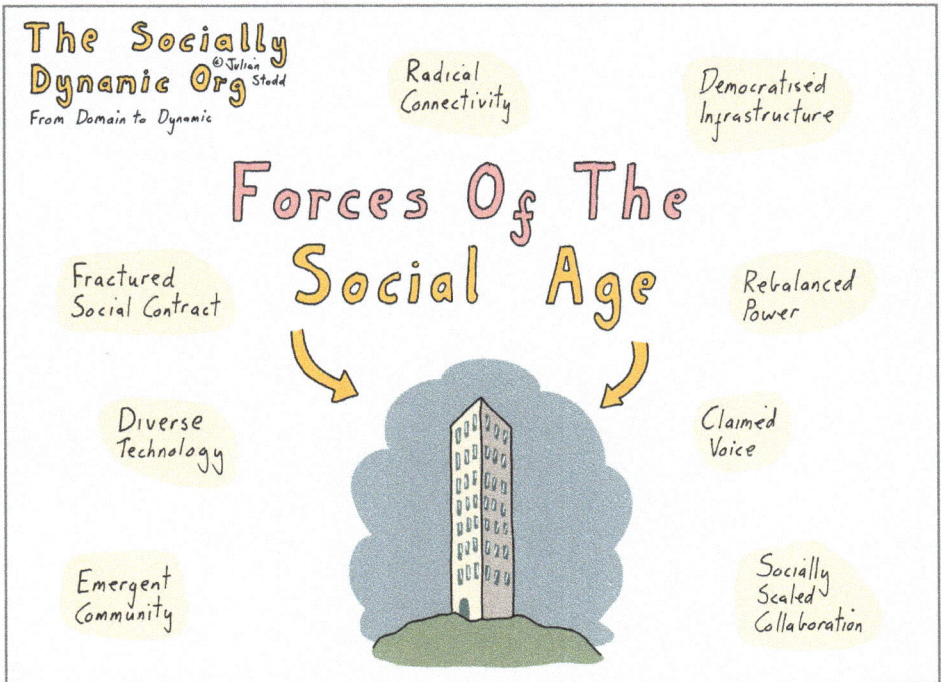

The Socially Dynamic Org © Julian Stodd
From Domain to Dynamic

Forces Of The Social Age

Radical Connectivity

Democratised Infrastructure

Fractured Social Contract

Rebalanced Power

Diverse Technology

Claimed Voice

Emergent Community

Socially Scaled Collaboration

I've written extensively about the context of the Social Age (see The Social Leadership Handbook and blog for an annually updated map), but to capture a few core tenets, we can see that this evolved ecosystem exerts pressure on the Domain-based Organisation in many different ways.

The fractured Social Contract means that '*Organisation*' is no longer the backbone of '*Career*'. Your social network, empowered at scale, is taking over that function, and increasingly, both learning and opportunity exist outside of the Organisation to which you are contracted. Similarly, your authentic leadership and Reputation-based power are validated outside of the formal structure, again at greater scale (and, hence, with greater resilience) than ever before. Essentially, we inhabit a parallel democratised infrastructure that enables us in many ways, almost all of which are beyond oversight or control.

I often lead a conversation about the Social Age by describing the radical connectivity we experience—again, almost all of which exists beyond formal oversight or control and with great resilience. And '*radical connectivity*' is not simply about remaining connected; it's a conduit of power, held in distributed Reputation and knowledge-based structures that differ from formal infrastructure, not simply in WHERE they exist, but in their multidimensional nature. HOW they exist: our social networks are multidimensional, in that we inhabit multiple different concurrent structures. (In the NHS, in our 2018 research, they inhabited '*belonging*' to an average of fifteen different communities that helped them to be effective on a daily basis).

This nature of connection also fosters a feature of Emergent Community whereby, in times of need, we are primed to aggregate into short-term communities of intent or interest. These may be transient, but they can be powerful and may not be purely consensus-based in nature but, rather, oppositional—in other words, communities that come together to oppose something, then disperse to be held as potential.

The diversified technology of the Social Age also exerts significant pressure on Organisations, which historically have viewed technology as a formally controlled aspect and, in itself, a mechanism of control. In our Landscape of Trust research, people describe how they '*trust*' formal technology around 30% less than they trust '*social*' tech. One emergent feature of this democratised availability and usage of technology is that weak voices can claim both space and volume. Instead of the printing press letting us print pamphlets to nail to the church door, we can create blogs, podcasts, subversive videos and viral communities at scale, all claimed as communities of intent.

A fundamental of the Social Age is the rebalanced power that this gives us—rebalanced, generally, in favour of the individual, and at the cost of the formal system. You can understand just about any system in terms of power, and the outlook for Organisations that rely on Hierarchy alone is bleak. Engagement is a currency that must be earned in the context of the Social Age.

In terms of Organisational focus, social collaboration is of great interest. It's seen as a way of mining the collective wisdom and brilliance of the people whom we have already hired. And it is, but there is a price to be paid, and we must understand the cost. It's typically paid in social currencies and through opportunity and access. Engagement is not something we can demand, so we need to learn how to earn it.

That's a snapshot of forces that impact the Domain Organisation, which is ill-equipped to respond. The issue is not that it lacks strength; it just holds the wrong type of strength.

What you need to know

The Social Age is a patchwork quilt of difference. It's the evolution of many aspects of our legacy bedrock that have eroded it to sand.

The ways that people are engaged in the Organisation, the nature and location of membership, the evolution of power itself, the increased desire and opportunity for individual expression and Reputation, as well as the more technological aspects of democratised capability, mean that someone can be innovative AND productive, without ever building an Organisation at all.

Questions to ask

1. What do you see that has changed? What does your map look like?

2. What have we lost?

3. What could we gain?

THE SOCIALLY DYNAMIC ORGANISATION
A New Model of Organisational Design

Part 3:

Codified Strength to Individual Agency

Let's consider why we need to move beyond the codified strength of the Domain Organisation and into a model of Individual Agency, connected at scale.

The Domain Organisation is tremendously strong when facing known contexts. But it is also typically curious about moving beyond this '*known strength*'.

As the forces of the Social Age erode historic power and re-contextualise legacy strength, we see increased interest in the language of agility and fluidity, sometimes expressed as an ability to change, to transform, to become '*digital*', to up-skill, to evolve.

All of this language means to be more fit, to be better, to be suited to this new context of the Social Age. But I contend that this is not simply a matter of known change in a known space. Instead, it's a matter of building a fundamentally new type of Organisation in a fundamentally new space— moving beyond Domain, to Socially Dynamic, by evolving the structure and mechanisms of the Organisation itself.

Consider '*Individual Agency*'.

The Socially Dynamic Org © Julian Stodd
From Domain to Dynamic

Not Codified Strength Alone

But Individual Agency At Scale

Agency is both the ability and the motivation to operate; it is your space to play. In that legacy Organisation, your agency was contextualised within a Domain and within a Hierarchy. You were limited by both power and space, but in the context of the Social Age, neither truly applies anymore.

We have agency, claimed socially, even if not granted formally.

When Organisations describe being more agile, having an ability to collaborate socially, to unlock the tacit and tribal wisdom of their Community, they are talking about Individual Agency and space to engage. But they do not always consider the price of this engagement and the factors that will drive it underground.

In the simplest language, Individual Agency is an ability to help shape the future space and the freedom to find a way to invest yourself within it.

So, it's a co-created model of change and a collaborative model of engagement.

The Socially Dynamic Org © Julian Stodd
From Domain to Dynamic

To Unlock Individual Agency

We Must Scaffold + Support

Not Own + Control

But to have this, we must foster the conditions in which it can occur: conditions of power, space, opportunity, structure and reward.

Factors like collaboration, creativity, innovation and agility do not happen in the abstract of the background context or in the absence of process or control. But the systems within which they take place may not be formally owned or moderated. So, even the most liberated individual is constrained by norms of culture and doubt, consequence and judgement.

Perhaps a useful language to consider is scaffolding. Scaffolding allows us to construct a building, but it is not the building itself. It enables.

If we want to unlock Individual Agency at scale, we may need to build out the scaffolding to support it, but not try to own it.

A Socially Dynamic Organisation will be scaffolded, not cemented, providing space within which people can invest.

What you need to know

The model of the Socially Dynamic Organisation is premised upon the idea of *'Individual Agency'*, scaled up. Essentially, it relocates the strength of the Organisation from assets into a dispersed community. (Well, it's not quite that simple, but it is a recognition of the potential to earn power at scale.)

Questions to ask

1. How does Agency operate?

2. How do individuals within your Organisation learn the limits of Individual Agency?

3. What is the role of Leadership in granting or tolerating Agency?

Part 4:

From One to Multi Dimensional

One way to view the evolution of Organisations is to understand it as a shift from one dimension, into many.

The first dimension is the formal Organisation: it's everything you can see and touch, as well as the formalised structures of power and consequence that surround it. So your employment contract, staff handbook, teams, equipment, products, IP, and customers.

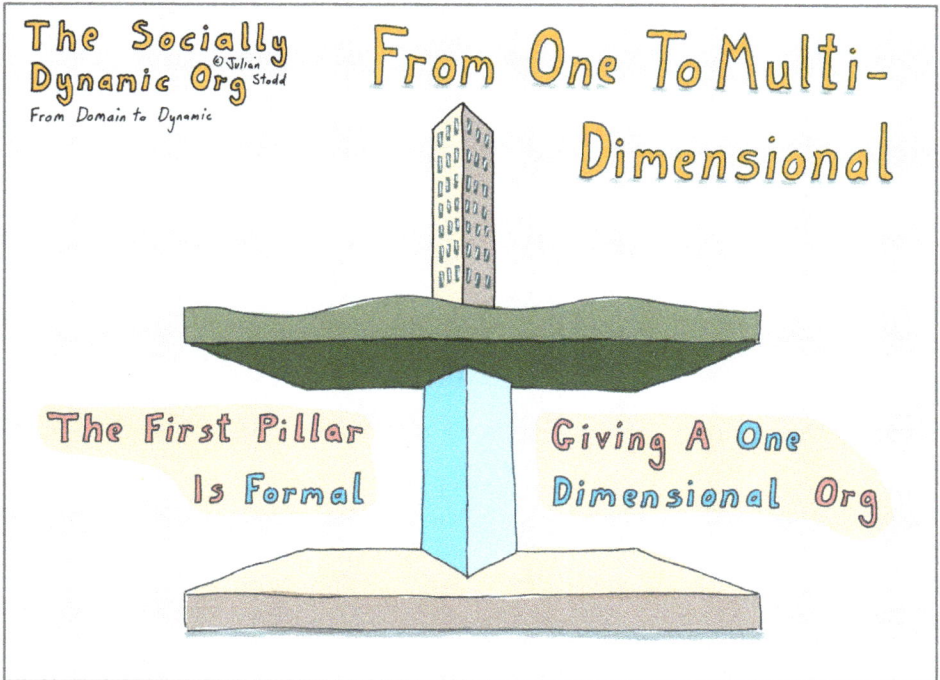

The proud history of our Organisations, and indeed the entire history of the Industrial Organisation with its Domains and legacy, built this first dimension.

But most of our Organisations today want to change: to be more agile, adaptive, creative, innovative, engaged, and dynamic. All of which involves building out subsequent dimensions.

The Socially Dynamic Org © Julian Stodd
From Domain to Dynamic

From One To Multi-Dimensional

Other Pillars Are Diversified Giving Additive Strength

Formal

Invested In Multiple Social Currencies

The change is not simply about structure, but rather about power and currency: the first dimension is built upon formal power and financial currency. Subsequent dimensions will be build on Social Authority, Invested Engagement, and Social Currencies.

Social Authority is power which is held within our communities, Reputation based authority. Invested Engagement is that which lies beyond the money we are paid for our utility. And Social Currencies are those that are traded beyond any exchange, and around the control of the Organisation: Pride, Trust, Gratitude, Respect, Reputation, Fairness, and Generosity amongst them.

I think that Organisations often get trapped into believing that the change they seek is the evolution of the first dimension, but it isn't: we need to keep that dimension, as it's one of our pillars that hold us safe and scaleable. Instead, it's about building out parallel pillars. Making us stronger, but more diverse.

So a Socially Dynamic Organisation will hold tremendous formal power, but also tremendous distributed Social Authority and power (only some of which will be held by formal leaders). It will doubtless have great formal structure (teams and domains), but also be highly socially interconnected, often through invisible tribes, networks and communities. It will have formal leaders, and social ones, who will sometimes (but not always), be the same person.

It can be liberating to view the future state in this way, because it allows us to avoid one particular trap: change means taking something away from people. Pride, empire, influence, power and so on. But in the multi dimensional model, change is more of an additive process, with the caveat that the things you may gain may need to be earned by the individual leader, not gifted by the Organisation.

THE SOCIALLY DYNAMIC ORGANISATION
A New Model of Organisational Design

Part 5:

The Porcelain Organisation

Domain Organisations hold great compressive strength, through their systems and process, Hierarchy and infrastructure, through their codified knowledge and institutional strength, through their great people, aligned to face a challenge that they understand well.

But, as we have already started to explore, the nature of that challenge is changing, and we need Organisations to adapt at the level of their very DNA: not a 'known change' to thrive within a 'known space' but, rather, to change in new and novel ways, to adapt to a challenge that is not yet fully understood.

This will be a tricky path to tread, because whilst needing a new strength, they must also maintain the best of the old, and therein lies the challenge. Much of the new strength operates beyond Hierarchy, trades in social currencies and is more of a dialogue than a broadcast monologue. Many parts of the 'new' will act in tension with the 'old'.

In my work and with my current understanding, I view that tension as a strength that we must exploit. If either side 'conquers' the other, we end up with an Organisation that believes it has 'the answer', at a time when we need Organisations that can be curious and constantly question.

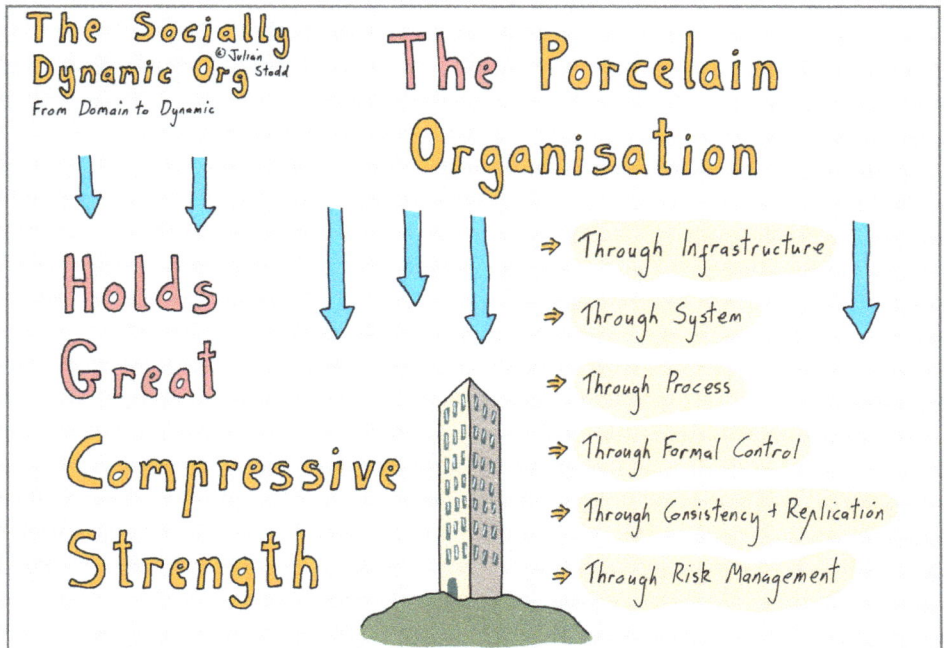

The Socially Dynamic Org © Julian Stodd
From Domain to Dynamic

Holds Great Compressive Strength

The Porcelain Organisation

⇒ Through Infrastructure
⇒ Through System
⇒ Through Process
⇒ Through Formal Control
⇒ Through Consistency + Replication
⇒ Through Risk Management

The notion of the Porcelain Organisation is one that lets us explore that challenge.

A Porcelain Organisation possesses great strength within that known space. Ceramics are hard, crystalline structures that can bear great weight. Running head-on into competition, into known markets, within well-understood regulatory and broader legal, financial and social structures, they can win. But, hit from the side, they can shatter.

The Socially Dynamic Org © Julian Stodd
From Domain to Dynamic

The Porcelain Organisation

Shatters Under Shock From the Side

⇒ Through Unmodelled Risk
⇒ Through Ambiguity
⇒ Through Asymmetric Shock
⇒ Through Market Fragmentation
⇒ Through Abstraction

What does this force look like—the force that can shatter an Organisation?

The forces of the Social Age, which I outlined earlier, are part of this: the fragmentation of career (hence, displacement of loyalty into emergent social structures), emergent community (hence, devolved and rebalanced power between formal and social systems), diversified technology (hence, weakening of formal infrastructure in favour of socially moderated, owned, and trusted channels). But, there is more: un-modelled risk (unknown unknowns), ambiguity (misunderstood knowns, contextual threats), asymmetric shock (giants toppled by innovative midgets), market fragmentation (where you end up trading in a new market for which you are maladapted), and abstraction (where the very premise of an old model becomes redundant—e.g. a taxi company or even a University).

Our risk-managed Organisations run on an assumption of understanding risk, quantifying it and mitigating it. And they often do, within the known space. But as Nassim Nicholas Taleb's work clearly demonstrates, it is the '*unknown unknowns*' that kill us, and risk modelling is a remarkably arrogant exercise. Much of the true risk is held in things that do not feel '*risky*' to a traditional Organisation. Look at Peloton, manufacturer of high-end exercise bikes, which, in late 2018, wiped 9% off its share value by tweeting a Christmas ad that ran counter to the empowered women's zeitgeist of the day.

Formal and hierarchical systems love certainty and kinetic action but cannot abide ambiguity (I have previously shared my broad research on this, in the writing on Black Swans and the limits of formal Hierarchy). But it is in ambiguity that we may find the weak voices that we need to hear. Indeed, many Organisations are currently working hard to try to unlock the power of this tacit, tribal, distributed wisdom, seeing it for what it is: a potential competitive advantage and root of innovation. So, their challenge can be seen as a quest for tidy answers in untidy spaces.

Asymmetric shock relates to rebalanced power. The blows that rain down upon the Organisation may not be hard, in the normal sense, but can stun us because they carry a different type of power. Authentic action can shock the Domain Organisation.

Underlying markets, the very conception and concept of Domains, is being challenged by new connective and democratising technology. Will notions of '*financial services*' or '*healthcare*' survive or be replaced by new organising principles? Many of our existing Domains describe utility, but we live in an age of experience. And, remember that Domains are part of that shadow cast into our past.

Related to this is Abstraction, which I explored in a broader article in 2018 on '*12 Modes of Failure*'. Abstraction is where the market takes an existing packaged offering and fragments it, extending the value chain and abstracting the original player into irrelevance. It's a slow death.

The attitude of many Organisations is to change in known ways. They understand the evolved context and need for change, but try to change on known terms, often terms that preserve existing structure and power. Many established consulting practices propagate this model, by offering '*known*' models of change at scale whilst being constrained themselves by heavy hierarchies that concentrate wealth and power at their peak.

To some extent, all Domain Organisations are Porcelain, because all are held within Hierarchy, structure, system and control. But, as I have said before, we will always need those things. Our challenge is additive and in tension. What do we need to add, and how will we hold the Dynamic Tension? Not to be safe as an end, but safe enough to survive, whilst being messy enough to learn.

So, we need a new type of Organisation, but not one that we can buy off a shelf—an Organisation that is not simply a tuning of the existing one, but evolution and a structural shift away from Domains.

What you need to know

All Organisations are Porcelain, but many do not understand exactly how. We need an additive strength and a Dynamic Tension. Our challenge may be to build an Organisation that can change in known ways but is adapted to learn how to adapt in new ones. And the answer will doubtless be grown from within, not bought from outside.

Questions to ask

1. Can you articulate your legacy strength, the specific mechanisms and structures that hold and support it?

2. Where are your Dynamic Tensions? How do you feel them or the pain of them? How do you or the Organisation respond?

3. Does your Organisation truly understand the signs of failure, and is it willing to listen to every voice?

THE SOCIALLY DYNAMIC ORGANISATION
A New Model of Organisational Design

Part 6:

The Organisation as Entity of Story and Belief

We are exploring the transition from Domain to Dynamic. The sections of this book collectively explore a new model of Organisational Design that moves beyond Hierarchy, infrastructure and control and into social collaboration, communities and Individual Agency at scale.

In my work over the last few years, I have come to describe this new type of Organisation, this adapted entity, as a Socially Dynamic Organisation, and in particular, I've been exploring how we will bring it into existence.

In that context, the notion of the Socially Dynamic Organisation has come to sit at the centre of what I do, alongside the parallel pillars of The Social Age, and Social Leadership. But my work and understanding continue to evolve; hence, this is a shadow of an answer, at best.

Some things are clear to me: that the new Organisation will be a product of both bold vision and leadership, coupled with Individual Agency at scale; that we will be more constrained from within than from outside; that most Organisations will fail to adapt at all.

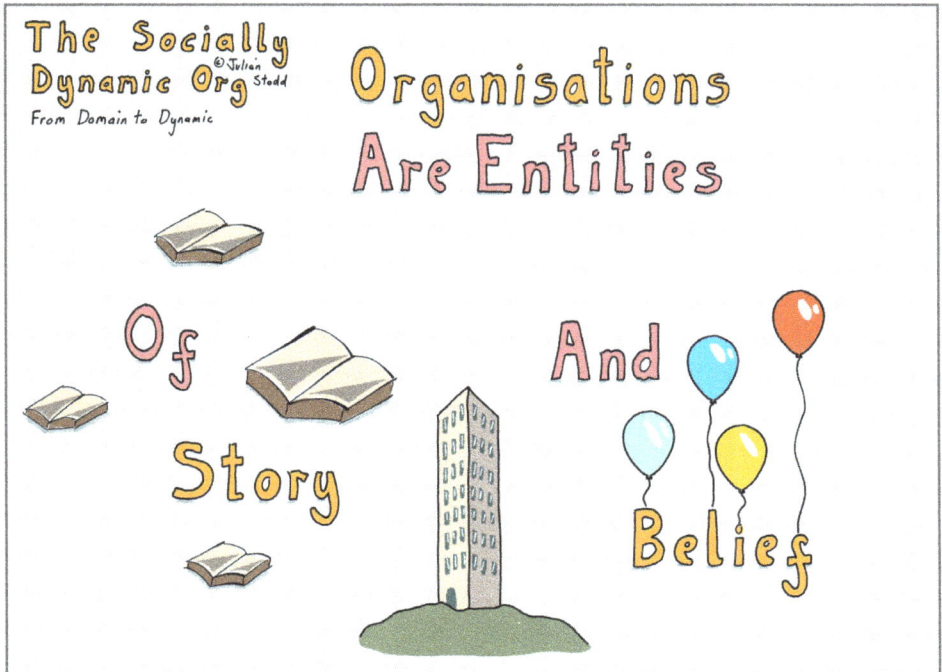

The Socially Dynamic Org © Julian Stodd
From Domain to Dynamic

Organisations Are Entities Of Story And Belief

But, more than anything, I have come to question the framework of change itself, landing in this new space. Change, of the sort that we require to build a Socially Dynamic Organisation, will be both structural and belief-based. We will have to invent the story, then see if anyone believes it and is willing to invest their belief in it.

At the start, I defined an Organisation as a mechanism of collectivism to achieve an effect at scale, and I looked at how it built '*domains*' to support this mechanism (and how everything else, from education to career, was shaped in this image). Next, we explored the context of the Social Age and the way that emergent forces act upon these Domain Organisations.

From there, I discussed how we can move from a notion of Codified Strength (held formally) to Individual Agency (held socially and individually). Then, finally, we considered the idea of the '*Porcelain Organisation*', one that holds incredible codified strength but shatters when rammed from the side by an emergent and un-modelled threat.

From here, we will look through a different lens. Many Organisations understand the need for change, and many are in the midst of large, complex and expensive efforts to adapt—for instance, from '*digital fitness*', through '*ways of working*', to '*social learning*', they can see a shiny future. But many will fail to reach it because they are locked into a structure of power, consensus and belief that will ultimately hold them back—good Organisations, full of good people but failing because they are structurally constrained (and often willingly so).

The route through this is to unhitch ourselves from these older structures: to disassociate power from position, to disconnect Hierarchy from place, to deconstruct infrastructure from control, and to understand that this process of loss is actually the foundation of gain. You cannot change without giving a great deal away, but the prize is even greater.

A Socially Dynamic Organisation is strong, not through infrastructure and formal power alone but, rather, through its people and the overlapping social structures that permeate it.

A Socially Dynamic Organisation is not simply an evolution into a new state; it is a parallel emergence into one—the best of the old, the best of the new.

Start with this position: an Organisation is a legal entity with possessions but also a series of stories. The '*things*' give a context of existence. Architecture in the physical domain segregates and sanctifies space, whilst both websites and social media profiles do similarly in the digital one, but without the context of a third spatial dimension. So, the phallic towers of Wall Street or Canary Wharf separate space and securely consecrate it, but the way we perceive them in culture, the stories we write about them, are where that power is held.

The very terms '*Silicon Valley*', the '*Bronx*', or '*Rust Belt*', apply both geolocation and context to power, as, indeed, to some extent, so do the domains .ac, .gov or .mil. But, in the model of parallel existence, there is the location, and then, there is the narrative. And, in the context of the Social Age, the narrative is the harder one to control, not least because it is not yours to control, and there is not one but many of them.

An Organisation is a story that it tells (its written history, its induction and onboarding story, its legal records and published work) and the story that is told about it (customer reviews, testimonials, urban myths, alumni narratives, media coverage, personal narratives).

But those narratives just set the scene. On the inside, the Organisation is an entity of belief held in the stories that are told by every one of its individuals: the job that they do, the Pride that they feel, the space (Individual Agency) within which they must operate. As I have said, stories carry within themselves a type of violence: they can empower and enable, or they can be imposed upon us as a limitation of space. They can constrain and control us, often by marginalising or characterising us in a way that is hard to counter.

So why is this web of storytelling important?

Largely because the move from Domain to Dynamic is not simply a formal transition in the physical realm; it is a transition of belief in the spiritual one! It is the fracturing of one narrative and the potential space for a new one to emerge. So, in this view, change happens both structurally and conceptually, at the same time, in the same space, but with one view imposed by formal power and the second one created collaboratively by the community itself, all underpinned by the individual narratives of every individual who forms part of the collective.

So, an Organisation is a collective belief: the story that it projects, the stories that are told about it, the consensual narrative of the internal teams and the individual stories of belief and space of operation, felt by every individual.

In this language, the way we build the Socially Dynamic Organisation is through story and belief.

I am most interested in the ways that Social Currencies, such as Gratitude, Pride, Trust, support this. All provide mechanisms by which we can invest and believe in the envisioned future state. So, perhaps I should add that the Socially Dynamic Organisation will be a story that we tell and in which we believe and can invest, through currencies that exist beyond money.

There is a clear dimension to all this that is worth unpacking further—namely, the way that change is most effective.

What you need to know

Organisations will need to change in known, structural ways, but also will need to be rewritten, into a story within which we can choose to invest belief. Really, this is about understanding how change happens: How much is held within the formal and legal system, the financial one? And how much is held in the culture itself, the social tribal structures and notions of belonging and storytelling?

Questions to ask

1. What does it mean to belong?

2. What are the currencies of belief?

3. Can you change if you lack a story in which to believe?

4. How is belief invested, and who controls the market?

5. How does this relate to social movements of change?

THE SOCIALLY DYNAMIC ORGANISATION
A New Model of Organisational Design

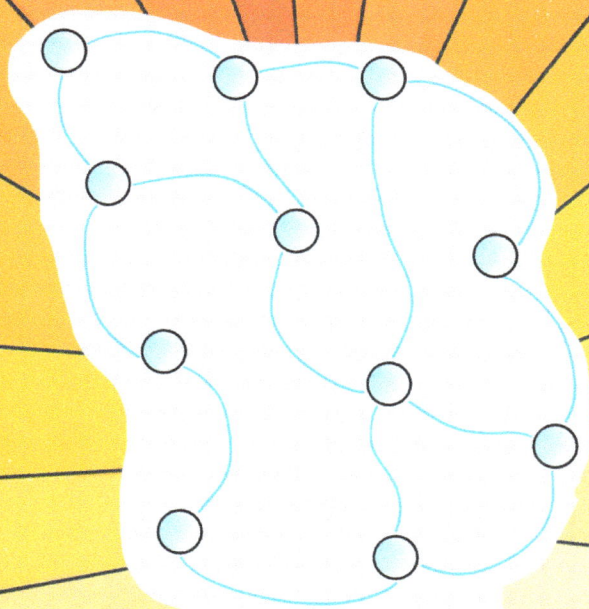

Part 7:

The Tension We Need

When I described the emergence and evolution of the Domain Organisation at the start, I described it in terms of physical collectivism and the invention of Hierarchy, system, process and control.

And, certainly, that is one way to view it: everything you can see, own and control forms the Domains of the Organisation—your legal contract, your company car, laptop, café, ceiling and floors, boxes and furnaces, trucks and logo. If you can quantify it and touch it, you probably own it. And Organisations are really excellent at making this stuff, expanding it and controlling it. Want a bigger effect? Build a bigger team and put someone new in charge. Hierarchy can expand forever, and you can never have too much stuff.

But, alongside the formal structure is a second one, harder to define clearly but significantly more important—the social structure that I used to describe as people, the networks of connection and Trust that flow within and around the formal structure. If you have an office and colleagues, the office is part of the formal structure, and the definition of '*colleague*' is held legally and contractually. But if you like them, trust them or are proud of them, if you would go one step further for them or protect them from harm or injustice, then you are describing the social structure.

Social structures differ from formal ones in both clear ways and more subtle ones. Whilst both could be described as being '*owned*', one is owned in a legal way and the other in a socially constructed one. You '*own*' your network of friends, in the sense that you can define it, carry it with you and, in theory, deconstruct it. But you do not own it in the sense of being able to rent it out or control it in a defined and repeatable way (although interestingly, in the context of the Social Age, I do define employment as rented access to individual agency and network, but that is a slightly different concept).

In the illustration, I describe the social structure as owning '*Community*', '*Engagement*' and '*Trust*', which is a bit of an abstraction. It's probably more accurate to say that it owns the social forces of a community and is where '*invested*' engagement sits. I define '*Invested Engagement*' in the Landscape of Trust work, as '*the extra mile*', engagement beyond the utility for which you are paid.

In some senses, you do not need to agree with my definitions of what sits in each '*bucket*', but I would encourage you to consider that certain things sit beyond contract and control or cannot be bought for money. Certainly, that is the central premise: there is both a formal and a social, system, and

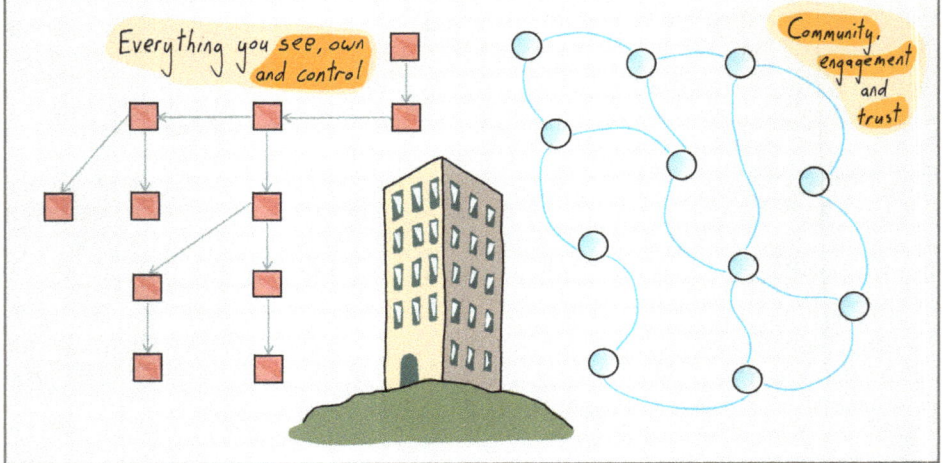

Intersection Of Formal & Social Systems: Context Of the Social Age

© Julian Stodd

Everything you see, own and control

Community, engagement and trust

interesting things happen at the intersection of the two.

But not smoothly.

The intersection is a challenging space, resulting in a Dynamic Tension, a tension that, if we ride it correctly, can power the Socially Dynamic Organisation, but which, if we get it wrong, can collapse it.

A more accurate description of a future state is not to consider the emergence of the Socially Dynamic Organisation as an evolution (in some ways) of the Domain Organisation, but rather a structure parallel to it. But, I normally do not make that so clear, because within that understanding lies a trap.

Many Organisations are trying to adapt within known parameters and structures of power and control. So, they almost make it, but they fail at the last hurdle. And failure is failure. So, the comfort of considering social dynamism as a parallel structure is a trap. But it's also true; neither can we afford to throw out the strength of the Domain Organisation.

Again, this is an abstraction, but broadly, it is fair to say that the Domain Organisation gives us structure, safety and scale, whilst the Social one gives us creativity, innovation and engagement (an imperfect definition, because, for example, safety is also a cultural component, hence, social. But, again, you can write your own boxes—just consider the principle for now).

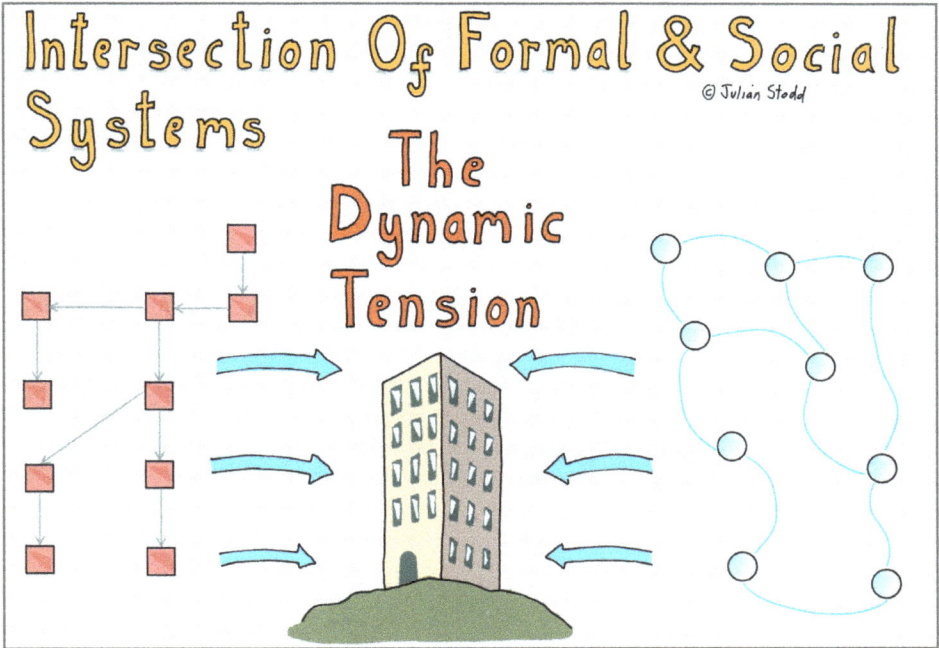

Intersection Of Formal & Social Systems
© Julian Stodd
The Dynamic Tension

I describe the Dynamic Tension as the tension between these two structures, and in an ideal world, we will maintain and thrive within it. Indeed, I would say that this Dynamic Tension is central to our ability to build a more Socially Dynamic Organisation. Without it, we may delude ourselves that we have changed but, in reality, we might only be repainting the walls.

I find that this is the most useful way to describe the situation. You already have a phenomenal formal structure, a Domain Organisation, which may thrive in yesterday's world. But we are all feeling the pain and the need for change, so you must build out a parallel structure—the best of the old, the best of the new. But, recognise that it is typically the old that kills off the new. Persistent structures of power and control, attitudes towards risk and, indeed, towards people prevent us from actually changing. In a very real sense, we are stuck in the present.

What you need to know

There are two systems—two Organisations, if you like—one formal and the other social. Different things exist within each one, and only the formal one is under your direct control. The Socially Dynamic Organisation will exist in a Dynamic Tension between these two worlds, allowing neither to fully subsume the other. This will be a tightrope to walk. Most Organisations fail because they fail to relinquish enough of the formal structure. Some fail because they relinquish too much.

Questions to ask

1. Do you understand how the two structures relate to your Organisation?

2. To what extent does your Organisation rely on formal, as opposed to social, mechanisms?

3. What would be the signs that the tension is collapsing?

THE SOCIALLY DYNAMIC ORGANISATION
A New Model of Organisational Design

Part 8:

The Responsibility of Organisations

Part of our exploration of the Socially Dynamic Organisation must consider the responsibility and underlying purpose of Organisations themselves—or so I would consider in my work. I may be adding my more liberal interpretation to the future Organisational Design Principles to which we should adhere, but that is for you to decide.

Possibly, one could construct a type of Socially Dynamic Organisation that is socially irresponsible or, more accurately, is socially exclusive, and so only acts fairly in selective spaces. But that is not what I am exploring here. My work would consider that an active responsibility of Social Leaders is to seek out quiet and excluded voices; hence, a broader responsibility of Organisations is to act globally in service of their societies and to navigate the frequent complexities of doing so in our ethically fragmented global context.

Clearly, there are multiple measures of success. You can generate profits for shareholders, provide opportunities for staff, be deemed to be deeply fair, do great good in the world. Money is the easiest one to measure, but that does not make it the most important, whatever capitalism tells us. And money is not mutually exclusive of the others, though it may require us to take a more balanced view.

Is wealth at the cost of fairness ever the right choice?

And if it is, then who will work the other end of the scale and build the society in which we want to live?

I've described this before, in terms of understanding a core question: does society exist to serve the Organisation, or do Organisations serve society? I don't mean that they exist as social enterprises or charities but, rather, that they act as corporate members of society with appropriate restraint and generosity to make society function.

In this illustration, I add the question of whether Organisations are a net drain on society, drawing fairness out and away, or do they act for net gain—are they able to be financially successful as well as deeply fair, contributing not only wealth but social good?

It's a matter of legitimacy. To act without responsibility is an affront to the legitimacy of the Organisation itself and to the Society within which it exists.

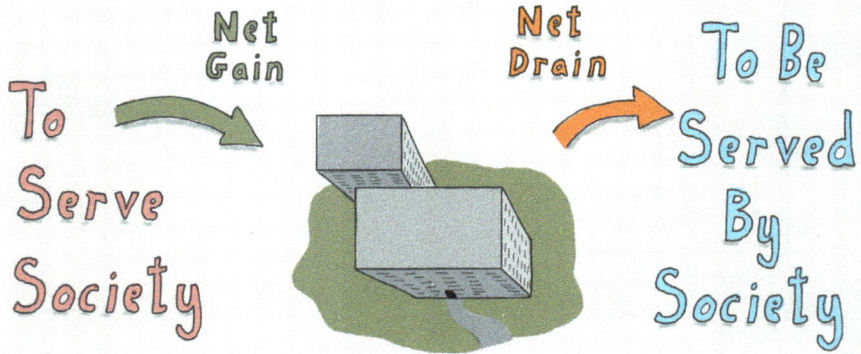

The Responsibility Of Organisations

© Julian Stodd

Net Gain

Net Drain

To Serve Society

To Be Served By Society

If you are thinking at this stage, '*just leave it to the market to decide*', then this writing is probably not for you; the market may well decide, but the market does not make any decision it adopts automatically '*right*'. If we add on a layer of fairness when we feel wealthy and fulfilled, but are willing to abandon it when things are tough, then we are charitable but unfair. Fairness is not about charity, not something to give away with discretion when we feel like it. Rather, it should be part of our core purpose and something that we invest for long-term gain.

So, should we sacrifice wealth for fairness?

What if the cost of that sacrifice is failure?

Partly, that's a disingenuous question: To wilfully fail is not fair either, not fair to staff or shareholders or, indeed, the wider society.

But the corollary of avoiding failure is not '*success at any cost*'.

It can be fair to make cuts, fair to make people redundant and even fair to make large amounts of money. But what may not be fair is to do those things beyond reason.

Cutting 10% of staff because that is your only sustainable option is one thing. Cutting because you think it's clever or makes you look like a six-shooting hero is not.

Cutting staff because you don't think they can learn, change, or contribute, is neither clever nor fair, and, yet, that is exactly what adulated industry titan Jack Welch did during his tenure at GE, with a legacy of '*forced ranking*' that permeated through industry more widely.

If we rely on markets to make us fair, we will fail. Markets do one thing well: impose transparent value on a system. If I would pay you ten dollars for it, then it is worth ten dollars. But fairness is not a directly traded currency, and even where it is traded, it is more honorific than fiscal. And, it may mean different things and be worth different amounts to different people.

I often play a game called '*Coins of Gratitude*' with people, in which they earn a coin to say '*thank you*' for things that are important to them. Sometimes those things are huge. I remember one man spending it on his partner for her care when he had been ill, and one young man spending it on his grandmother, who had funded his MBA in international development, helping him to achieve his dream of helping others. Other people are grateful for small things, like their dog or chocolate. But all just earn one coin. The value of that coin is socially imbued and unique to each person. Fairness is a little like that.

I can act however I like, but I cannot make you think it is fair.

But if I act fairly towards you, you will know it.

So, fairness is contextual, judged in the receipt and rarely traded, existing beyond money.

At the end of the day, we will have to invent and narrate the Organisations that we want, if we are not to be caught in the service of the Organisations that we deserve.

We will have to invest fairness if we want Organisations to be fair.

And we will have to put down our heroes of old and find some new ones who have earned the respect that we invest in them.

We can be wildly successful by being wildly fair. And, certainly, we do not have to write people off to be successful.

So, consider the Organisation you inhabit, and ask where it is responsible: to you, to shareholders, to wider society. And answer the same question for the Organisation that you are building: is it fair, and in which direction does that fairness face?

And, ask if it is draining or acting for Society's gain. Is it successful to serve— to create opportunity and act as a force for good, to reinforce and refresh society through progressive approaches to labour, the environment and reward? Or, is it successful just to make money by selling people out?

This is the responsibility of the Socially Dynamic Organisation, and it carries us into aspects of Organisational Design and effect that may historically have been limited to the narrow view of Corporate Social Responsibility or even Public Relations.

What you need to know

The Socially Dynamic Organisation will carry a broad remit for fairness: to individuals, the company and the wider society. These scales may sometimes be hard to balance.

Questions to ask

1. Are we fair now? How will the future outcome be similar or different? Relate this to both policy and behaviour if you can.

2. In your own words, describe the responsibility of the Organisation that you wish to build.

3. Can you identify a socially responsible Organisation? How is that responsibility held and experienced?

Part 9:

The Socially Dynamic Organisation

In this section, I attempt to provide an overview of how this new type of Socially Dynamic Organisation will look.

This is a sketch, and one that I have reworked several times; the value of sketches is that we can redraw them, we can learn and amend them. The main value it may bring is if it provides us with something to which we can relate all action.

Organisations are good at being busy, but they can fail if they fail to align action to a central premise. If we want a more Socially Dynamic Organisation, then we will need to build it, but to build it requires more than just busy action. Using your own sketch, you can try to ensure that there is a thread that runs through everything.

It's easy to be busy. It's very hard to actually change.

The Socially Dynamic Org © Julian Stodd
From Domain to Dynamic

Trusted and Trusting

Interconnected Beyond Hierarchy

Guided not Governed

Changeable by Design

Lightweight and Reconfigure-able

Constantly Curious

Strong Social Leadership

Fair by Default

Resilient Through Humility

A Socially Dynamic Organisation

'Guided not Governed'—A central realisation is that our future Organisations will be less about the governance of hard power and more about the workforce's invested engagement, discretionary effort and willing support. Essentially, those Organisations that thrive will do so because of the engagement and energy of a highly connected population that has elbow room and space to operate. In that sense, the role of leadership will shift from one predominantly of governance, to one of facilitation and enablement or guiding. We could argue that good leaders have always done this, which is true, but in the aggregate, the experience of employment has typically and ultimately been one of subservience to the system. In the future, it is more likely to be predominantly about choice and investment.

'Trusted and Trusting'—These are two very different aspects of this complex social force. Domain Organisations have excellent structures of formalised Trust, through contract and Hierarchy, but are not necessarily trusted at scale and do not necessarily demonstrate trust in their actions (or, at least, do not do so with consistency, a requirement of trust for many people). The Socially Dynamic Organisation will excel at Trust for several reasons. First, it will trade in multiple Social Currencies, not just one financial one (understanding Social Currencies is central to understanding the Social Organisation). And, it will understand that Trust is contextual and held primarily through authentic action. So, it will excel at creating space for authentic action!

'Interconnected Beyond Hierarchy'—Within the Domain Organisation, Hierarchy carries power and control but can separate us tribally and globally. Interconnectivity is an important notion to follow—the ways that we engage not simply into known spaces but also unknown ones, not simply in comfortable ones but across our differences, too. The word *'interconnectivity'* is one of the most important to explore in our efforts to understand and build more Socially Dynamic spaces. It is through stronger interconnection that we can build social movements and unlock Individual Agency globally on a local scale.

'Strong Social Leadership'—I have described how our challenge is to keep the best of the old and unlock the best of the new. So, alongside the formal power that allows us to achieve an effect at scale sits the social authority that enables us to safely invest. Social Leadership is Reputation-based authority; the Socially Dynamic Organisation will have both strong formal leaders who earn high Social Reputation and strong Social Leaders who carry no formal power at all. This is because building this new Organisational design will require us to give up many of the things we currently own, such as power, position, resources, control. We will have to hold people safely as we do, and Social Leaders will enable it to happen.

'Lightweight and Reconfigurable'—Our future Organisations will be less overweight than our current ones; most likely, they will employ fewer people but perversely touch more people to be effective, through distributed networks and stronger associate and affiliate arrangements and within the arms of broader communities. The Social Age represents an age of community, and it is likely that successful Organisations—certainly globally successful ones—will operate something akin to a citizenship model in this space—reconfigurable because they will not simply construct a new Domain but, rather, retain a constant ability to change.

'Constantly Curious'—This ties into the notion of the restless Organisation, one that does not seek one mode of operation, codifying it into system and process but, rather, develops a deep-seated ability to solve complex problems in diverse ways. Essentially, whilst the Domain Organisation was effective through simplification and codification, the Socially Dynamic one will be effective through iteration and innovation, remaining in constant motion. To do so is much harder than it seems; excellent Organisations become constrained simply through the accretion of system and process around things, bogging them down over time. Being restless, constantly curious, is hard and will most likely involve a methodology around curiosity that enables it to scale.

'Fair by Default'—Most Organisations can act fairly when they wish to, but the Socially Dynamic one will be fair by default. In other words, it will have to go out of its way to hurt people because the communities that it serves will hold the mindset and authentic power accountable. That may sound like some liberal and aspirational statement, but in the world of interconnection, Trust and Social Authority, it's vital. By creating a culture of fairness, we can better hear weak voices, better engage and just simply invest in our society, rather than cost it.

'Resilient through Humility'—I am linking two disparate concepts here: resilience, and humility. Through our willingness to be wrong and learn from it, to engage in spaces of difference and dissent and to reach out to carry heavy weights with others, we can develop greater Organisational resilience—not in the hard construct of infrastructure and network but, rather, in the social ones of culture and ideas. The humble leader is one who puts others first, invests even when they have little and shares widely.

'Changeable by Design'—Whilst Domain Organisations change through pain, the Socially Dynamic one will be able to do so by design, simply because it

will never fully root itself in the current space. This is one of the hardest tricks to fulfil. Social systems inherently nest in formal spaces, forming tribes and enclaves. If we avoid nesting, we can be changeable by design. But it's more than that; it's about a recognition that true change is co-created and allows everyone to both envisage and invest in the future state, which really relates back to the first point of '*guided, not governed*'.

These are just a light scattering of the traits that we see in a Socially Dynamic Organisation, and none of them is that hard to build in isolation. But isolated strength will not suffice. It's about a systematic pattern of adaptation, which is what makes it so hard to build.

My work is simply a sketch of this space, with a focus on the practical ways that we adapt, but nobody is going to give you your answers. Each individual, each Organisation, each leader and each community will need to find their truth. My premise is taken from models of evolutionary biology: as the ecosystem changes (i.e. the full context of the Social Age comes to bear), we must either adapt or fail. Better to adapt.

What you need to know

The Socially Dynamic Organisation is holistically adapted. Much of that adaptation takes place beyond clearly codified systems and formalised rules, but this is really what we should expect. The formal system has carried us a long way, but the context of the Social Age opens a new space of operation, and it's a space of competitive advantage if we are willing to be fair and share the rewards, as well as the hard work. The Socially Dynamic Organisation is something to be earned.

Questions to ask

1. What would be your first step in building this?

2. What will be your biggest challenge?

3. How will you know if you are making progress?

4. Where will your first Community space for change be?

5. Who will lead, and who would you follow?

THE SOCIALLY DYNAMIC ORGANISATION
A New Model of Organisational Design

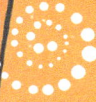

Conclusion:

Pick Up Your Hammer

This book explores the context and the idea of the Socially Dynamic Organisation. We have looked at how the Social Age has applied pressure to the old model, and how the future requires new types of strength. I hope that one thing has been clear: both our older Domain Organisations and the newer Socially Dynamic ones are populated by good people doing good things.

We are not thwarted in our efforts to conceive and visualise the future state but, rather, are constrained by our ability to socialise and build it. We are constrained by the very structures (both formal and social) that we inhabit today.

Change is often about loss—a loss of status, power, prestige or empire; a loss of certainty or community; a loss of identity or seniority; the loss of Hierarchy or control. It's sensible to fear losing some of these things but, in reality, what we have to gain is far greater.

The Socially Dynamic Organisation is multidimensional. It has both formal and social structures, and we can find both power and identity within both.

But the heart of the challenge is this shift from the one-dimensional Org to the multidimensional one. The other dimensions are different—and sometimes weird.

In these pages, I have provided the lightest-weight guidance through just some of the forces and factors that will impinge upon our thinking and impact upon our efforts.

It's like we have a jigsaw before us, but all the parts are face down. We know it's a jigsaw, but we are uncertain of what the picture will be.

The takeaway from this book should not be a single piece of knowledge, and there is certainly little wisdom within it. Rather, I hope that you take away restless energy and renewed intent.

Shake the pillars, question the foundations and be prepared to do the heavy lifting to build the thing anew.

Remember: Our Organisations are entirely made up. Every aspect of power, every mechanism of effect, every structure of control, all are made up, and all can be deconstructed and rebuilt stronger. More relevant. Fairer. Better.

That's the work. Pick up your hammer and get building.

The Socially Dynamic Organisation

© Julian Stodd

THE GUIDEBOOK SERIES

I've written a series of *'Guidebooks'* for the Social Age: these cover aspects of my work that are still rapidly evolving, or which I have not made time to write a full book about yet. They are typically under 10k words, and are intended to provide an overview of the landscape. I try to keep them practical, with a key highlight on *'what you need to know'*, and *'what you can do about it'*.

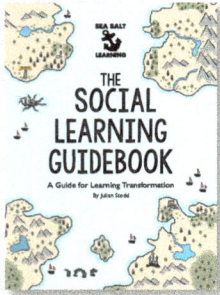

The Social Learning Guidebook

Provides a practical overview for the principles and design techniques of Social Learning in a modern organisation.

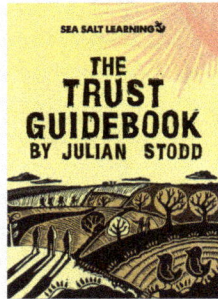

The Trust Guidebook

Explores our extensive research into the Landscape of Trust, and asks 72 questions that leaders can use with their teams.

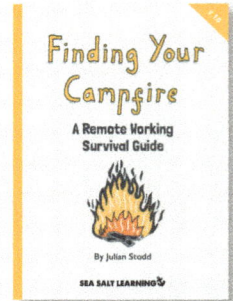

Finding Your Campfire

This short book is a survival guide for individuals, teams, and organisations navigating the experience of remote work.

Quiet Leadership considers the Organisations that we inhabit as an ecosystem, and the way that none of us can tend to the whole of this system alone. Only by connecting at the most local level, through the smallest of actions, can we weave a strength into our culture, and keep the ecosystem healthy at scale.

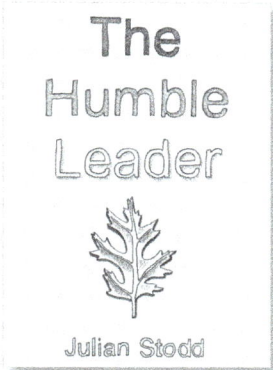

The Humble Leader is a guided reflection into our personal humility as a Social Leader.

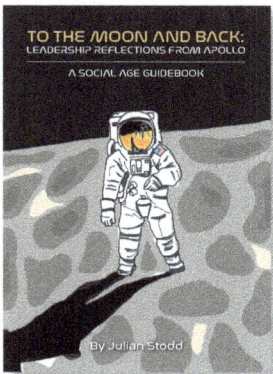

To the Moon and Back: Leadership Reflections from Apollo shares eight key stories about the Apollo programme, alongside my personal reflection on what this means for Leadership in the Social Age.

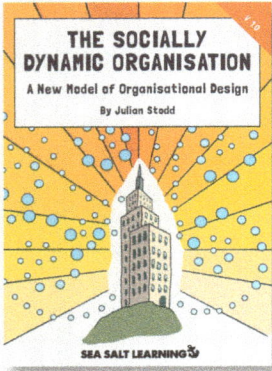

The Socially Dynamic Organisation
For a new type of world, we will need a new type of Organisation: one that is lightweight and rapidly adaptable, that thrives in times of constant change, that respects the old but embraces the new.

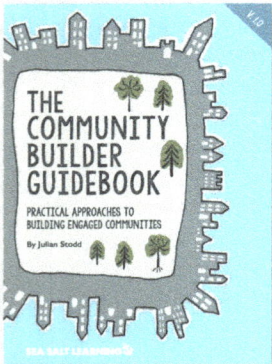

The Community Builder Guidebook brings you practical ideas to create engaged and dynamic Social Learning Communities and Communities of Practice.

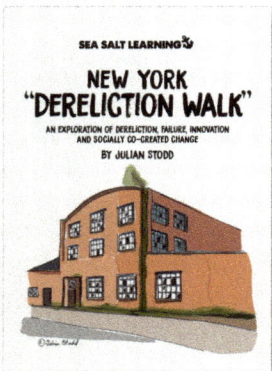

The New York Dereliction Walk is more experimental work, exploring how Organisations and ideas fall derelict and fail, but can be reborn through social movements. It was my favourite writing from 2018.

THE HANDBOOK SERIES

'Handbooks' are intended to capture a full snapshot of my evolving body of work on a particular subject. 'The Social Leadership Handbook', now in its second edition, explores the intersection of Formal and Social authority, and considers the importance of this in the context of the Social Age.

I'm currently finishing writing 'The Change Handbook', which is an exploration of how Organisations change, and the forces that hold them constrained. It considers how we build more Socially Dynamic Organisations.

THE '100 DAY', & 'SKETCHBOOK', SERIES

Whilst *'Handbooks'* and *'Guidebooks'* are about ideas and strategy, the *'100 Day'* books tackle how we do these things at scale. They do so by providing a scaffolded space, which you can explore, document, and graffiti, as you go.

'Social Leadership: My First 100 Days' is a practical, guided, reflective journey. It follows 100 days of activity, with each day including provocations, questions, and actions. You fill in the book as you go. It's accompanied by a full set of 100 podcasts.

'The Trust Sketchbook' is another guided, reflective journey, a walk through the Landscape of Trust, but in this case you graffiti and adapt the book, to capture your own landscape.

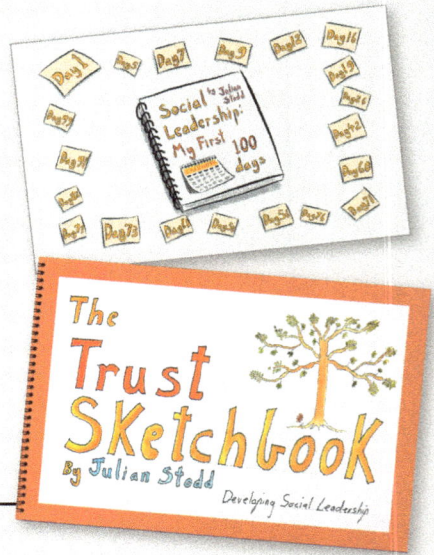

OTHER BOOKS

I have written a series of other books, covering aspects of learning, culture technology, and knowledge, which you can find details of on the blog.

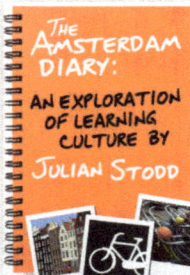

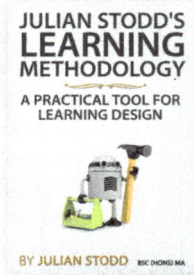

CERTIFICATIONS

In 2018 I launched the first Certification programme on *'Storytelling in Social Leadership'*. It's based upon *'Foundations'* and *'Techniques'*, which are practical and applied, and *'Experiments'*, which you learn to run in your own Organisation.

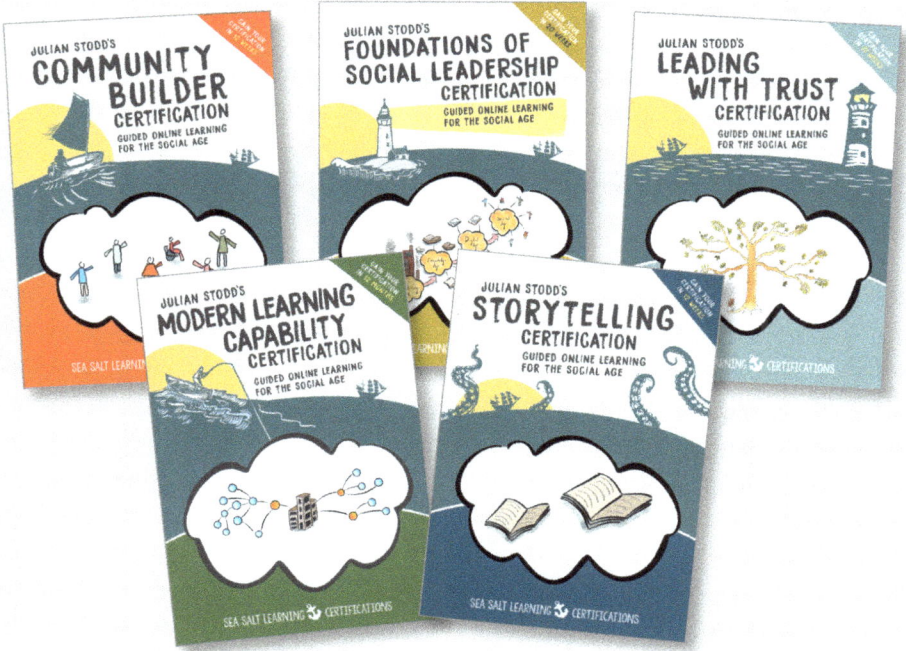

'Storytelling in Social Leadership'
'Leading with Trust'
'Community Building'
'Foundations of Social Leadership'

'Modern Learning Capabilities'
'Leading Through Change'
'Social Age Navigation'

Get in touch to find out more
www.seasaltlearning.com/certifications

SOCIAL LEADERSHIP DAILY

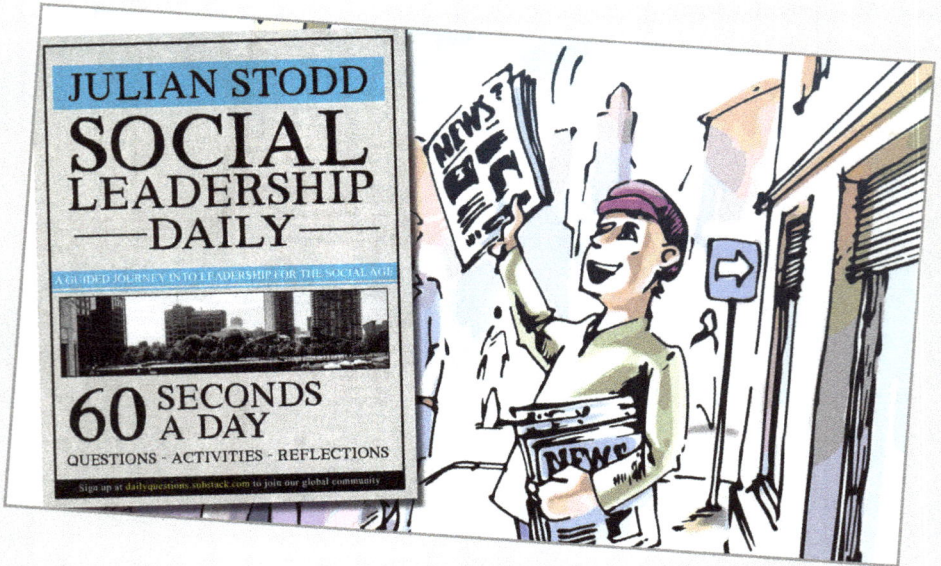

Daily questions, activities, and reflection in the arms of a global community of Explorers, putting Social Leadership into their everyday practice.

dailyquestions.substack.com

ABOUT SEA SALT LEARNING

We are a dynamic *Social Age startup:* living the values we speak. We are virtualised, global, inclusive, and agile. We are a core team of around twenty Crew Mates.

We are surrounded by a much larger layer of Social Age *'Explorers'*, people who are heavily involved in *'sense making'* around our core topics of Social Learning, Social Leadership, Change, Culture, and the Socially Dynamic Organisation.

Sea Salt Learning builds upon the work by Julian Stodd, author and explorer of the Social Age, recognised for his pioneering work in helping organisations to adapt to the new reality of the Social Age.

The *Sea Salt Research Hub* carries out original, creative, and large scale research, providing an evidence base for our work.

Sea Salt Publishing provides a curated body of books and online publications, exploring all aspects of the Social Age.

Sea Salt Digital provides our technical capability and build capacity for eLearning, mobile, video, and other forms of online learning.

Notes

Notes

www.ingramcontent.com/pod-product-compliance
Lightning Source LLC
Chambersburg PA
CBHW040930210326
41597CB00030B/5246